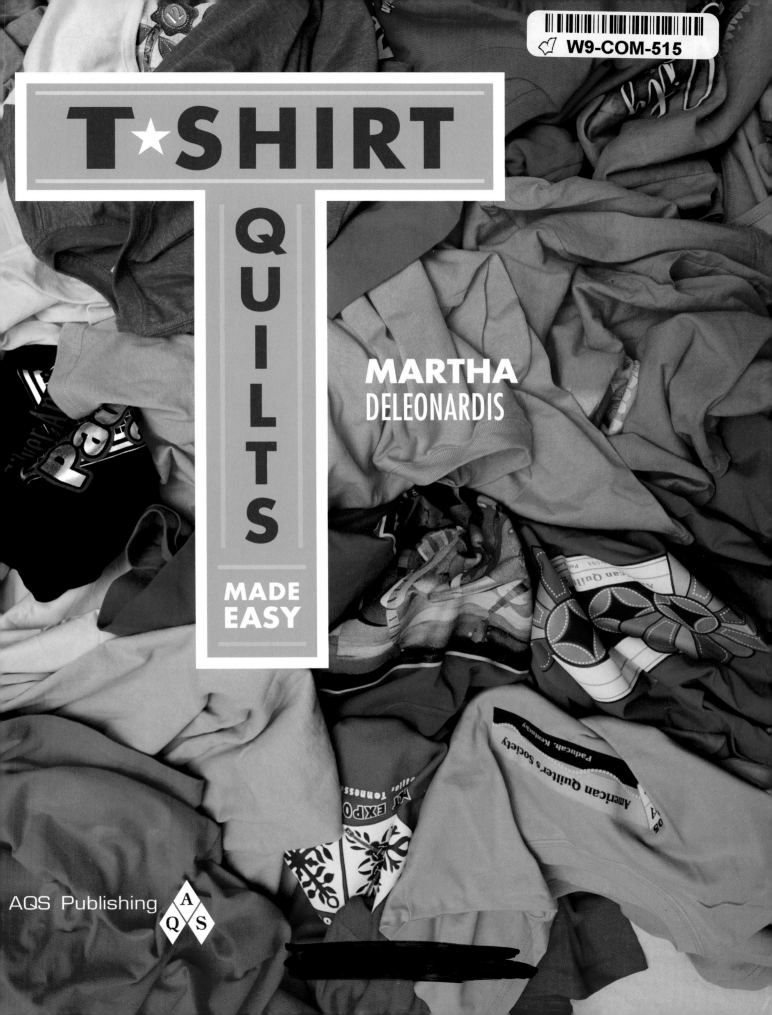

# T★SHIRT

## QUILTS

### MADE EASY

**MARTHA** DELEONARDIS

AQS Publishing

Located in Paducah, Kentucky, the American Quilter's Society (AQS) is dedicated to promoting the accomplishments of today's quilters. Through its publications and events, AQS strives to honor today's quiltmakers and their work and to inspire future creativity and innovation in quiltmaking.

Executive Book Editor: Andi Milam Reynolds
Senior Editor: Linda Baxter Lasco
Copy Editor: Chrystal Abhalter
Graphic Design: Lynda Smith
Cover Design: Michael Buckingham
Quilt Photography: Charles R. Lynch

Additional copies of this book may be ordered from the American Quilter's Society, PO Box 3290, Paducah, KY 42002-3290, or online at www.AmericanQuilter.com.

Text ©2012, Author, Martha DeLeonardis
Artwork ©2012, American Quilter's Society

Library of Congress Cataloging-in-Publication Data

DeLeonardis, Martha.
  T-shirt quilts made easy / by Martha DeLeonardis.
    pages cm
  ISBN 978-1-60460-014-8
  1. Patchwork--Patterns. 2. Quilting--Patterns. 3. T-shirts. I. Title.
  TT835.D4515 2012
  746.46--dc23
                    2011048772

# Acknowledgments

Allow me to thank the following people:

Terri Burton: For inviting me to teach at Quilt 'n Sew, my first professional quilting gig. Thank you for the opportunity, encouragement, and support.

Dianne Labunky: For putting little bugs in my ear, as well as the many T-shirts donated to the cause.

Mindy Kossmann: For the baby T-shirts and making sure needed supplies were always available.

Roberta Addington: For access to your great stash of T-shirts as well as editing advice.

Angela Rodgers: For your photographic talent.

Debra North and Justin Bauman: Thanks for allowing your quilts to be included in this book.

All my sisters in quilting: Dorothy Bieman, Sharon Collins, Pat Conner, Joy Denk, Evelyn Eason, Anna Gallagher, Ruth Grimes, Venetta Hilton, Pam Lanham, Kathie LeBoeuf, Michelle Mitchell, Sherri Moore, Karen Morrison, Noella Mukherjee, Brenda Oenbring, Tineke Pots, Caroline Tan, Jennifer Thacker, Sue Werner, and Leslie Yale—for endless encouragement, brainstorming, as well as help sewing sleeves and labels onto quilts. I could not have completed this manuscript in the short time frame without your help. Go "A" team.

Special thanks to Pellon for providing the fusible interfacing and batting for Quilt City.

Last but not least, a special thanks to my husband, Ralph. Without your support over the years I would not have been able to pursue my love of quilting.

Cover quilt: QUILT CITY, detail. Full quilt on page 47.

# Table of Contents

FANGS 2 U, detail. Full quilt on page 28.

# Introduction

It *is* possible to make great looking quilts from ugly T-shirts—what I call "Cinderella" quilts. The essence of a Cinderella design is a strong desire for one's eye to travel freely over the entire quilt composition. An asymmetrical design infused with a variety of fabrics is a sure-fire way to achieve this.

When I first started making T-shirt quilts, the freeform asymmetrical design method I used was somewhat complicated (see JUSTIN'S T-SHIRT QUILT and SERENDIPITY in the Gallery, pages 43–44). This complexity was not an issue until I started to teach T-shirt classes. Wanting to present to my students with more simplified construction methods while continuing to produce quilts with that Cinderella look, I developed numerous easy-to-make asymmetrical T-shirt quilt designs. I have included one traditional sashing design (SAFARI SASHED, page 34) to demonstrate that a Cinderella quilt can also be created using a symmetrical design. Fabulous fabrics are essential to pull off this design (see It's All About the Fabric, page 6).

I have included some unique projects—items that might not usually be associated with T-shirts—specifically baby T-shirt quilts and T-shirt pillows. I hope these projects inspire you to think a little differently when doing laundry; maybe not all the clothes will end up back in their drawers.

It has become a tradition in my family for me to make each graduate a T-shirt quilt from their high school shirts. Grandma's gift to the graduate is a large dorm pillow incorporating a collegiate T-shirt. Pillows are great gift ideas. You might only have time to make one T-shirt quilt for a special graduate next spring, but pillows could be made for all your gift giving.

Many of the projects in this book have been designed to utilize manufactured precuts—5" Charm Squares and 2½" width-of-fabric (WOF) strips. By taking advantage of manufactured precuts, you will obtain fabric pieces from a complete line of fabric. This is an economical way to infuse large numbers of different fabrics into a project, while at the same time speeding up the construction process by reducing time spent cutting—a win/win in T-shirt quilt construction. All the baby T-shirt projects can be made with pre-cuts.

One of the inherent problems encountered when making T-shirt quilts is the variation of image sizes to be utilized as T-shirt blocks. Several projects in this book address this issue. In addition, Design Opportunities (page 14) shows how odd-sized T-shirt blocks can be modified for inclusion in quilt designs that require a specific size T-shirt block. The Quilt Design Chart (page 49) will help you determine which design method will best meet the existing variables of your quilt project.

I know from personal experience that it is one thing to cut up someone else's T-shirts and use an objective eye to design a Cinderella quilt. It is quite another thing to cut up your own loved one's T-shirts, because there are many rite-of-passage memories associated with them. I have some guidelines to help with this process.

You do not have to incorporate every T-shirt that

has ever been saved. If you need to use most of them, think about a second quilt, or maybe incorporate some in the border (see HOTTEST BRAND RUNNING in the Gallery, page 41).

You are the designer! If you are making this quilt for someone special, do not consult with them beyond cleaning out the T-shirt drawer and inquiring about their favorite color. If you do discuss the quilt with them and later regret it, preface informing the troublesome party of your intended design plan with "The book said I should…."

HAVE FUN! Don't sweat the small stuff. This is not an heirloom project. You are making a quilt that should be lovingly used, and used, and used.

## *Note to Novice Quilters*

Basic quiltmaking information not covered in this book is readily available though many venues. Beyond books and magazines, today's beginning quilters are blessed with unlimited opportunities for learning over the Internet. A quick search will produce many videos on unlimited subjects. My only caution is to view several on the same subject to be sure you are getting accurate information.

FANGS 2 U, detail. Full quilt on page 28.

# Hints and How-To's

## Tools and Notions

The basic quilting tools needed for T-shirt quilts include:

Rotary ruler—6½" x 24" or 6" x 12"

Rotary cutter and cutting mat

Scissors

Marking pens

Iron

Sewing machine in working order and basic sewing supplies

12½" x 12½" square ruler—a must-have for T-shirt quilts

Pressing cloth, non-stick appliqué sheet, or Bo-Nash Iron Shoe (See Resources, page 62.)

T-shirt quilt construction requires no special notions; general purpose thread and Universal needles are adequate. I personally always piece using Aurifil™ 50-weight thread in gray, white, or black, and a size 70 sharps needle. Keep your machine happy; always clean your machine and replace the needle before starting a new project.

## It's All About the Fabric

The three most important factors in creating a gorgeous Cinderella T-shirt quilt are fabric, fabric, and fabric! The more fabrics included in each quilt, the better!

When purchasing fabric remember the old adage: you get what you pay for. Higher quality fabric will produce a better end product. Not only will your quilt look better, but also higher quality fabric will make the construction process easier. Please patronize your local quilt shops before looking for your fabric elsewhere; as quilters, it is in our best interests to keep these establishments open for business.

T-shirt color should not be the focus when selecting fabrics. Let me say this again—ignore the colors of your T-shirts when deciding on a color scheme. You could end up with a convoluted collection of fabrics of every color in the rainbow if you based your fabric selection on the color of your T-shirts. Thinking that the fabrics should match the T-shirts is where many quilters run into problems. When this doesn't work they resign from the design process and pick one or two neutrals that will not clash with any T-shirt, resulting in a lackluster quilt.

The solution is to select a color scheme as described below; then when laying out your blocks, place coordinating fabrics around the different T-shirts for a pleasing composition.

There are several ways to approach selecting fabrics for your project:

Use a focus fabric.

Use precuts or fabrics from one fabric line.

Utilize color theory.

Choose a theme.

Usually value is a very important design consideration in fabric selection. In T-shirt quilts this is not the case. The value of most T-shirts to be incorporated in a quilt will vary significantly enough that it usually is not a concern in fabric selection.

## Focus Fabric

Select fabrics for your quilt that coordinate with a chosen focus fabric. If you are unsure if colors of different fabrics match, refer to the small dots printed on the selvage of your fabrics. These are the actual colors used in the printing process. SERENDIPITY (page 44) is an example of a quilt where fabrics were selected around a focus fabric—the outside border. You might not think to use all these fabrics together, but they all work because all the fabrics coordinate with the focus fabric. More often than not, the focus fabric is used in the border but this is not a rule. In JUSTIN'S T-SHIRT QUILT (page 43), the focus fabric is the large multicolor circular fabric used in the body of the quilt.

## Fabrics from One Line

Fabric manufacturers hire designers who have been trained in color theory to design fabrics. Take advantage of this knowledge by choosing fabrics from a single line, or use precuts. There are a number of projects in this book that use pre-cuts (Charm Squares and Jelly Rolls) including all the baby quilt projects.

## Color Theory

Another method for selecting fabrics for your project is to utilize color theory. This is not hard; you learned this in elementary school. If you dress yourself in the morning, you can do this! Don't be afraid. If my engineer brain can figure this out, you can, too. In T-shirt quilt design it is best to keep things simple. There is already a lot going on within the T-shirts themselves. Therefore, simple non-complex color schemes generally work well.

Monochromatic—using one color
Analogous—using colors next to each other on the color wheel.
Complementary—using two colors that exist opposite each other on the wheel.

You will notice that the fabric color scheme of many of the quilts in this book is black and white with the addition of one other color. This is essentially monochromatic, as black and white can be classified as non-colors. This color scheme works especially well in T-shirt quilts and is a great option for a quilt made specifically for a guy. Speaking of making quilts for the males of our species, batik fabrics are another great choice. More and more precuts are becoming available in batik fabric lines.

When an analogous color scheme is used, choose a variety of color hues. Leanna Darling requested modern blues and purples in her quilt. I used some twenty odd fabrics in ISN'T THAT DARLING! (page 40) that ranged from turquoise to magenta. Varying hues within a color causes the fabrics to play off of each other creating sparkle, thus producing a more interesting design.

For more information on fabric color theory, there are a number of great books authored by formally trained quilt artists. Some of my favorites are listed in Resources (page 62).

## Theme

The last method of selecting a color scheme would be to go with a theme—music, sports, cowboys, etc. The only caution is to watch that the colors within the chosen fabrics coordinate fairly well.

## Cutting and Stabilizing T-Shirts

### Stabilizers

Any iron-on interfacing product can be used to stabilize T-shirts because they just need to be stabilized until they are sewn into the quilt. I recommend 911FF Pellon® Fusible Featherweight, a non-woven iron-on interfacing, because it is very forgiving. The manufacturer's instructions do not have to be followed precisely, which is not the case with many iron-on interfacing products.

### Colored Interfacing

If you are incorporating a jersey into your quilt, you may need a colored iron-on interfacing so the stabilizer does not show through the little holes of the jersey weave. There are black and gray products on the market. If your local quilt shop does not carry a variety of interfacings, they are readily available in big box fabric stores. Take the jersey with you when shopping so you can audition and select the best color interfacing for your shirt.

# Hints and How-To's

## Cutting and Stabilizing Children's and Baby T-Shirts

To preserve the maximum surface area of small T-shirts, use scissors to cut down the back, then across the top back of the sleeves. Neck facing and sleeve seams may need to be ripped to access maximum shirt surface.

When working with baby onesies, pull the bobbin thread for fast removal of stitches.

Stabilize the T-shirt using iron-on interfacing. Cut a square of interfacing roughly 2" larger than the dimensions you want to cut your T-shirt. Place the

T-shirt right-side down on a pressing surface and press. Place the interfacing adhesive side (bumpy side) down on the wrong side of the T-shirt. The straight-of-grain (non-stretch direction) of the interfacing should run across the T-shirt. Fuse following the manufacturer's instructions.

Place the T-shirt right-side up on a cutting mat. Center a square ruler over the printed image on the T-shirt. Cut to the desired dimensions. If necessary for a more centered T-shirt block, cut slightly above the neck fabric so a sliver of interfacing peeks out. This omission of T-shirt fabric will be hidden in the seam allowance.

## Cutting and Stabilizing Adult T-Shirts

Using rotary cutter and ruler or scissors, cut up the sides and through the sleeves of the T-shirt. Next, slice the shoulder seam. This will expose the maximum surface area for stabilizing.

Since vertical length above the printed image is usually desired, do not cut off the neck band. If your T-shirt needs to be cut 18½" wide, cut according to the instructions for cutting a child's shirt.

Place the T-shirt right-side down on a pressing surface and press. Center an 18" wide piece of iron-on interfacing on the wrong side of the shirt, adhesive-side down. (For T-shirt blocks to be cut 18½", cut your interfacing 21" wide.) The straight-of-grain (non-stretch direction) of the interfacing should run across the T-shirt. The top edge of the interfacing should cover at least part of the neck facing. Fuse following the manufacturer's instructions.

## Trimming T-Shirts into Blocks

Place the T-shirt on a cutting mat and center a 12½" square ruler over the printed image. Cut to the desired dimension using a rotary cutter. Because most rulers have ½" increments on one side and 1" increments are on the opposite side, caution needs to be taken when centering the image. I count in from both sides of the ruler to the image edge in increments.

If you are making a quilt using many blocks of a specific size, say 4" or 6", you may want to purchase a smaller square ruler. If you want a T-shirt block larger than your ruler, use the lines on the cutting mat in conjunction with your ruler to trim the T-shirt to the desired size. Remember—measure twice, cut once!

## T-Shirts and Beyond

You can use more than just T-shirts in your quilts. Sweatshirts, team jerseys, and even a sports towel from your favorite team can be incorporated in a quilt.

## *Piecing Hints*

Generally, you use a "shy" ¼" seam allowance when piecing to make up for the slight loss of dimension when seams are pressed to one side. A greater loss occurs in T-shirt quilt construction due to the thickness of the T-shirt fabric. Therefore, instead of a "shy" ¼" seam, a "bashful" ¼" seam allowance keeps dimension accurate. Instead of aligning the raw edges of the T-shirt and fabric, move the T-shirt ever so slightly so just a peek of fabric is showing. Use the edge of the fabric as a guide to sewing the seam.

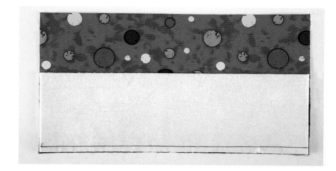

Because T-shirts are stabilized across the horizontal, when sewing horizontal seams, the T-shirt should be the top fabric as it is moving under your sewing machine's presser foot. When sewing vertical seams, position the T-shirt on the bottom.

Always press seams away from the T-shirts, not open.

When sewing Grid Method sections together, you will encounter T-shirt-to-T-shirt seams pressed to one side, as well as long seams with multiple T-shirts where seams will need to be pressed in opposite directions. Snip the seam allowance so the seams will lie flat.

If you are encountering difficulties sewing two T-shirt fabrics together, attach an even-feed or walking foot to your machine.

## Hints and How-To's

Use a Teflon® iron shoe or cover the T-shirt with a non-stick appliqué sheet or pressing cloth when pressing the seams to protect the image on the T-shirt.

Use little tag-sale stickers or blank ink jet labels to keep small notes and dimensions on cut T's.

## *Incorporating Curves into T-Shirt Quilts*

Having a circular or oddly shaped printed image on a T-shirt presents an opportunity to incorporate curves into your project. It is best to follow the curves in the printed T-shirt when drawing your cutting line. Because most images printed on T-shirts are slightly distorted, chances are that the cutting line will not be a symmetrical circle, but this is OK. Ovals also work well using this technique.

There are two techniques I use to incorporate curves into T-shirt quilts. A tweaked Sharon Schamber Piec-liqué machine curved-piecing method works best with smaller images–circles 4"–6". With larger images, I like to use a slight variation of Wendy Hill's Easy Bias-Covered Curves technique. Bias strips are topstitched over the outer edge of a T-shirt that has been basted to a background fabric block. FANGS 2 U (page 28) contains examples of both techniques.

## Bias Strips over Appliqué

Special Tools and Supplies:
Clover® ½" Bias Tape Maker
Aerosol spray starch or sizing
18mm rotary cutter
Water soluble marker

Bias Strip Fabric:
²/₃ yard for circle diameters 11½" or less
¾ yard for circle diameters larger than 11½"

Make your fabric work for you! Using stripes or plaids for bias strips will add interest to your project.

Using the 45-degree lines on your cutting mat and ruler, cut 1" wide bias strips. Cut and join as many strips as needed to make a single strip the length required.

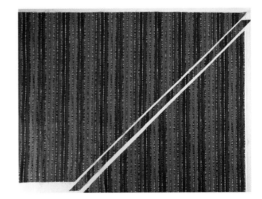

Spray the strip with sizing or starch.

To help guide the bias through the tool, insert a straight pin through the slit on top of the bias tape maker, then hold the tip of the bias with the pin as the maker is pulled away from the end of the strip. Press the folded bias as it emerges through the bias tape maker.

Cut the background fabric 1" larger than the desired finished block dimensions.

Prepare the T-shirt image per the instructions in Cutting and Stabilizing T-Shirts (page 7).

Draw a cutting line 1"–2" beyond the image on the T-shirt. I like using a blue water-soluble marker; this allows flexibility in adjusting the cutting line. Using scissors or an 18mm rotary cutter, cut away the excess T-shirt fabric.

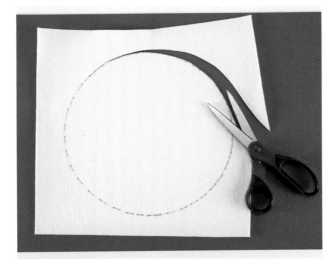

Pin the T-shirt to the right side of the fabric background and baste along the edge.

Pin the bias over the basted edge of the T-shirt, leaving the blunt-cut bias end loose. Overlap the bias ends 1". Blunt-cut the excess bias fabric. Remove several pins for ease of joining the bias ends.

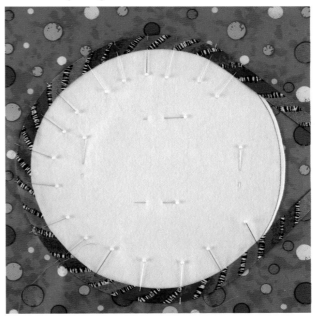

Cross the ends of bias (similar to how binding is finished), pin, check that the strips are not twisted, and sew corner to corner.

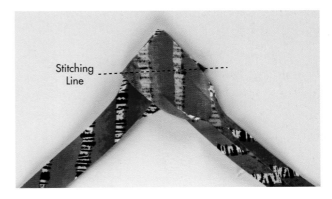

Snip the seam allowance and press the seam open to reduce bulk. Press the bias edges down.

Re-pin the bias. Topstitch the outer edge, removing pins as you go. Topstitch the inner edge. Press.

If the background fabric's printed pattern is noticeable though the T-shirt, with wrong-side up, trim the fabric away from behind the appliquéd T-shirt.

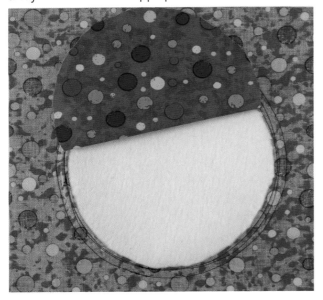

Trim the block to the desired dimension.

## Machine Curved Piecing

Special Tools and Supplies:
Aerosol spray sizing or starch
Twin pencils—two regular pencils taped together
Foam brush and plastic cup
Basting glue
Freezer paper
18mm rotary cutter

Prepare a small T-shirt image (4"–6") according to the instructions in Cutting and Stabilizing T-Shirts (page 8).

Cut the background fabric 1" larger than the desired finished block dimensions.

Draw a finished-size circle on freezer paper.

Using an 18mm rotary cutter, cut out the circle, leaving a "frame."

Iron the freezer-paper frame onto the wrong side of the background fabric.

Using the double pencil, draw both sewing and cutting lines on the inside of the circle, close to the paper.

Remove the paper. Apply a thin line of basting glue to the seam allowance, close to the folded edge.

Center the fabric right-side up over the T-shirt image.

Press to set the glue.

Sew on the fold/pencil line.

Using the small rotary cutter, cut the fabric on the inside line, creating the seam allowance. Snip the seam allowance.

Spray sizing/starch into a paper cup. Dab a brush into the liquid and apply to the seam allowance. Press the seam allowance back against the paper.

Trim the excess T-shirt away from the seam allowance. Press.

Trim the block to the desired dimensions.

## Design Opportunities

It is inevitable that at times a cut T-shirt will be too small for the dimensions required for a particular project, but there are a number of things that can be done to remedy the situation.

The simplest solution is to frame the too-small image with fabric to reach the desired size.

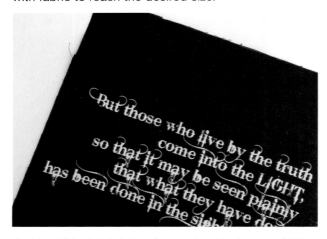

*A strip of black fabric has been added to the top of this T-shirt motif.*

This can be done with complementary fabric (see TWISTIN' FUN, page 36); with fabric very close in color to the T-shirt; or even with a leftover piece of T-shirt.

See Piecing Hints (page 9) for advice on piecing two T-shirt fabrics together.

*A piece cut from the same T-shirt was added to the top and bottom of the sewing machine motif.*

Other solutions for a too-small block or image:

Sew several small images together or combine them with fabric to create a larger block.

*Two rectangular motifs were joined to form this block.*

*Two small motifs and two fabric squares were combined for this Four-Patch block.*

Incorporate an image within a circle (see Incorporating Curves into T-Shirt Quilts, page 10).

Appliqué a T-shirt image onto fabric. This can be done within a block or even on a border. Imagine numbers from jerseys and T-shirts randomly appliquéd onto a border. Very neat!

## Machine-Appliqué Hints

Trim the stabilized T-shirt image to the desired shape.

Place tear-away or cut-away stabilizer beneath the shape (NOT the fusible you used to stabilize the T-shirt) and the background fabric.

Set the zigzag stitch width to 2.5 and the length to 0.8. This is somewhere between a satin and zigzag stitch. Machine appliqué the image in place.

Remove the excess stabilizer.

*Stabilized appliqué motif stitched onto background fabric*

## *Finishing Touches*
## Topstitching Interfaced T-Shirts

To prevent interfacing from ever separating from a T-shirt block, topstitching can be applied to permanently secure these two materials together. This technique is advantageous when the T-shirts will not be quilted over, as in a quilt that is tied or in a T-shirt pillow. This step is not necessary on a machine-quilted T-shirt quilt.

Before incorporating the stabilized T-shirt into a quilt, mark quilting lines on the interfacing side of the block. Use a ruler to draw a line through the diagonal center of the block, then draw lines on either side of the line 1½" apart. I use a water-soluble marker, misting with water to remove the lines when finished.

*Draw lines on interfacing side.*

*Stitch from the interfacing side using bobbin thread to match the T-shirt.*

## Flat Welting

Inserting flat welting is a great technique for adding that little extra zing. The illusion of an additional border is especially advantageous when making smaller quilts. I incorporated flat welting into JUNIOR TWIST (page 22).

After most of the borders had been cut and sewn on, I decided it needed an additional inner border out of the light green fabric. Using a flat welting saved me a huge hassle. I just detached the sewn borders, added the welting, and I was on my merry way to completing the project.

*JUNIOR TWIST, detail. Full quilt on page 22.*

Measure the center of the quilt in both directions; use these dimensions to cut welting lengths. Use these dimensions to determine border lengths as well.

Cut a 1½" wide strip of fabric. Fold in half lengthwise, wrong-sides-together (like a binding), and press. Cut to the length of each of the four sides of the quilt top.

Align the raw edges of the flat welting with the raw edge of the quilt top. Baste with a $^1/8$" seam. (Basting might cause the quilt top to gather slightly, but after the borders are attached, the quilt will lie flat again.)

Repeat on the remaining three sides. Then attach the border strips with a ¼" seam.

## Alternative Machine Binding

Traditionally, bindings are machine sewn to the front of a quilt and anchored to the back with hand stitching. There is an alternative method for attaching a binding without any handwork. This is an excellent method for finishing a T-shirt quilt. Not only is this method faster, substituting hand stitching with machine, it increases the durability of the quilt.

Cut binding strips 2½" wide.

Follow traditional instructions for piecing the strips:

Sew the binding to the BACK of the quilt with a ¼" seam, turning corners and joining the ends as you would for a traditional, hand-finished binding.

Turn the binding to the front, pin, and topstitch the edge in place with a straight or decorative stitch.

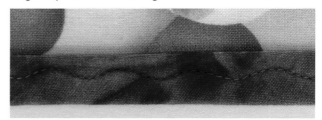

*A serpentine stitch secures the binding while adding a decorative element to the edges.*

## *Quilting Recommendations*
### Batting and Backings

To be properly quilted, backing and batting need to be larger than the quilt top in both directions. T-shirt quilts are very heavy, so use a thin cotton batt such as Warm & Natural. Do not plan on incorporating T-shirts into your backing. Again, the quilt will be too heavy to use comfortably, and chances are a longarm quilter will not accept it for quilting.

## Quilting

I recommend quilting T-shirt quilts on a longarm machine. T-shirt quilts are heavy and unless you are quite competent quilting on your domestic machine, it will be well worth the expense of having it quilted by a professional longarm quilter.

Talk to your longarm quilter before purchasing backing and batting. Each longarm quilter will have personal preferences to consider. To load onto a quilt frame, backings need to be significantly larger than quilt tops.

If you don't know any longarm quilters in your area of the country here are some ways to contact one.

- Talk to your local quilt shop staff. If they do not have a machine on premises, they may know of professional longarm quilters in your area.

- Contact your local quilt guild. If your local guild publishes a newsletter, longarm quilters will often advertise there.

- Perform an Internet search of longarm guilds in your state. They can provide a listing of their members.

- Investigate the ads in the back of quilt magazines.

## Tying

Tying a T-shirt quilt, rather than quilting it, is another option for completing your project.

HOTTEST BRAND RUNNING, detail.
Full quilt on page 41.

# Sugar & Spice

36" x 42", made by the author

This quilt is Jelly Roll friendly. For a second design option of cutting Jelly Roll strips into squares, see FROGS AND SNAILS AND PUPPY-DOGS' TAILS in the Gallery (page 42).

## Fabric Requirements

15–19 T-shirts*

3 yards iron-on interfacing

8 precut 2½" WOF strips

⅓ yard for the inner border

1¼ yards for the outer border and binding

*If you are using images from both the front and back, you'll need fewer T-shirts.

## Checkerboard Squares

Sew 2 contrasting 2½" WOF strips together lengthwise. Press toward the darker fabric. Sub-cut into 2½" segments.

Cut 6 – 2½" WOF strips into various sized segments as specified in the following chart:

| Length | # Segments from each strip |
|--------|----------------------------|
| 2½" | 6 (36 total) |
| 4½" | 4 (24 total) |
| 6½" | 1 (6 total) |

## Quilt Construction

Stabilize the T-shirts as instructed in Cutting and Stabilizing T-Shirts (page 7) and trim to dimensions divisible by 2 plus ½" (2½", 4½", 6½", 8½" etc.), whichever dimensions are appropriate for each shirt.

Note how many of each T-shirt block size you have in the 2" Grid Cut Block Chart (page 50). Divide the T-shirt blocks into three groups.

If you have Electric Quilt® 7 software, construct a three-column grid to plan your layout.

If you do not have design software, use the 2" Block Set Guides (pages 55–58) in the Easy Planning Guides chapter to plan your layout. Audition placement of the T-shirt blocks in the design. Change the width and length of the block set as appropriate for your T-shirt collection.

As an example, my Block Set Guide for SUGAR & SPICE is shown below.

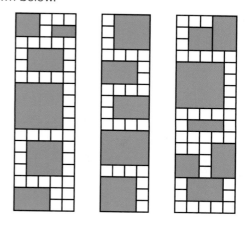

Following your Block Set Guide, lay out the T-shirt blocks on a design surface and audition placement of the fabric segments. To camouflage the column construction, place previously constructed checkerboard segments on either side of adjoining columns. Be sure to continue the checkerboard pattern from one column to the next.

Sew fabrics and T-shirt blocks together to create each column. Press the seam allowance away from the T-shirts when joining fabrics to T-shirts. Press fabric-to-fabric seams in the direction that will create nestled seams when subsections are sewn together.

Sew the columns together.

Measure through the center of the quilt in both directions to determine the length for the borders. Cut 1½" wide strips for the inner border. Cut 3½" wide strips for the outer border. Add the borders to complete the quilt top.

Quilt as desired.

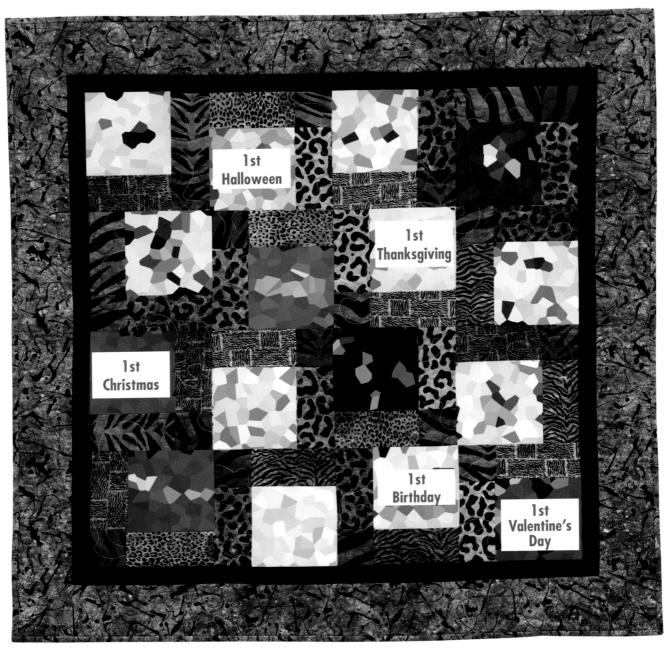

# Logan's Shirts of Firsts

34" x 34", made by the author

This split Nine-Patch is constructed with 5" x 5" squares. This is an excellent
cut dimension when using baby T-shirts. Faster construction can be achieved by
using precut Charm Squares. All the T-shirt blocks need to be the same size.

Design Hint: One strong fabric used consistently in the center of all the
Nine-Patch blocks (the purple zebra print in this quilt) will liven up the design.

## Fabric Requirements

16 baby T-shirts*

10 or more ¼ yard cuts of various fabrics
(or precut Charm Squares); 2½ yards total

2 yards iron-on interfacing

¼ yard Nine-Patch center squares

¼ yard for the inner border

½ yard for the outer border

⅓ yard for the binding

*If you are using images from both the front and back, you'll need fewer T-shirts.

## Quilt Construction

This quilt is made from 4 Nine-Patch blocks that are cut into quarters and rearranged.

Stabilize 16 baby T-shirts as instructed in Cutting and Stabilizing T-Shirts (page 7). Center the printed image under a 5" x 5" area on a square ruler and trim the T-shirts to measure 5" x 5".

Cut 4 – 5" squares for the Nine-Patch block centers.

Cut 16 – 5" squares from the remaining fabrics.

Make 4 Nine-Patch blocks with 4 T-shirt squares in the corners and 5 fabric squares. Don't overly obsess when determining placement of the T-shirts. The placement will be altered when the blocks are sliced and rearranged.

Press the seam allowance away from the T-shirts.

Cut Nine-Patch blocks into 4 sub-blocks as follows:

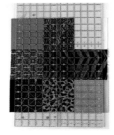

Use 2 rulers to find the center of the block.

Remove one ruler.

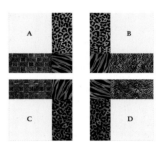

Slice the Nine-Patch vertically. Repeat horizontally.

Label the 4 sub-blocks as shown.

Separate the sub-blocks into groups A, B, C & D. Audition placement of the sub-blocks as shown below.

Join the sub-blocks into rows and sew the rows together.

Measure through the center of the quilt in both directions to determine the length needed for the borders. Cut 1½" wide strips for the inner border and 3½" wide strips for the outer border. Attach the borders to the quilt top. Quilt as desired.

# Junior Twist

32" x 32", made by the author

This twist and turn project is a great option for making a baby quilt. The flexibility of the T-shirt size increases the pool of shirts available to be incorporated into this quilt. This design is Jelly Roll friendly.

For this project T-shirt sizes can vary slightly. The cut dimensions of the T-shirt blocks used in this quilt ranged from 5¾" to 6¾".

## Fabric Requirements

9 baby T-shirts*
1½ yards iron-on interfacing
9 assorted 2½" WOF strips
¼ yard for the flat welting
¼ yard for the inner border
1 yard for the outer border and binding
*If you are using images from both the front and
    back, you'll need fewer T-shirts.

Special Tools for this project: 8½" x 8½" square ruler

## Quilt Construction

Stabilize the T-shirts as instructed in Cutting and
Stabilizing T-Shirts (page 7).

Place each shirt right-side up on a cutting mat. Center
the image under a 6½" x 6½" area on a square ruler
and trim the T-shirts to measure 6½" x 6½".

Cut 2 – 6½" and 2 – 10½" segments from each 2½"
WOF strip. (Adjust the cut segment lengths if any
T-shirts vary from the 6½" size.)

Sew the 6½" segments to the
sides of each T-shirt square.
Press away from the T-shirt.

Sew the 10½" segment to the
top and bottom of the T-shirt
square; press away from the
T-shirt.

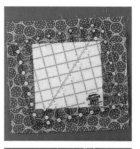

Lay an 8½" square ruler on
top of the block twisting it to
the **left**.

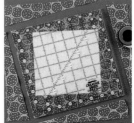

Trim.

Repeat for a total of 5 blocks
with the center image angled
to the **right**.

Twisting the ruler to the **left**
gives you a block with the
image angled to the **right**.

Trim the remaining 4 blocks with the ruler twisted to the
**right**, resulting in the center images angling to the **left**.

Arrange the blocks in 3 x 3 block setting, alternating
the twists.

Sew the blocks into rows, pressing the seams in
opposite directions in alternate rows.

Sew the rows together, pressing the seams in one
direction.

Measure through the center of the quilt in both directions
to determine the length needed for the borders.

Follow the instructions in Finishing Touches (pages
15–16) to make flat welting.

Cut 1½" wide strips for the inner border. Cut 3½"
wide strips for the outer border. Attach the borders to
complete the quilt top.

Quilt as desired.

# Grid Method Quilts

Amy Bradley Designs  www.amybradleydesigns.com
Block Party Studios  www.blockpartystudios.com
Greater Houston Area Shop Hop
West Houston Quilter's Guild
Quilter's Guild of Dallas

# Charmed Journey

64" x 86", made by the author, quilted by Quilt 'N Sew Studio, Katy, Texas

Using fabric squares in a standard grid is a great method for incorporating T-shirt blocks of differing dimensions into an asymmetrical quilt design. Turning a grid design into a Cinderella quilt only requires infusing the project with many fabrics. CHARMED JOURNEY, FANGS 2 U, SCAVENGER HUNT, and QUILT CITY were all assembled using this Grid Method.

This construction technique works best using a four-inch, six-inch, or Charm Square size (5") grid. The question is, which size should you utilize?

If you fall in love with a Charm pack line of fabric, then of course you will use the 5" size. In doing so, you will save time using these precut squares. If you decide to cut your own fabrics squares, I recommend using the four-inch or six-inch grid; both are fat-quarter friendly. As illustrated in the chart below, the dimensions for cutting T-shirt blocks when using Charm Squares are not numbers quilters regularly use.

| Grid Size | Finished T-Shirt Dimension Options | Cut T-Shirt Dimensions |
|---|---|---|
| 2" | 2", 4", 6", 8", 10", 12", 14" | 2½", 4½", 6½", etc. |
| 4" | 4", 8", 12", 16" | 4½," 8½" 12½", 16½ |
| 5" (Charm Squares) | 4½", 9", 13½", 18" | 5", 9½" 14", 18½" |
| 6" | 6", 12", 18" | 6½", 12½", 18½" |

If you are cutting your own squares, deciding between the six- or four-inch grid will depend on which of these two formats is the best fit for the unique T-shirt dimensions in your project. The six-inch grid is the more efficient size; its larger format requires less cutting and fewer seams. In contrast, the four-inch grid is more flexible having four size options as opposed to three in the six-inch grid.

Another option is to use a fabric Jelly Roll with a 2" grid. Baby T-shirts work really well in the smaller grid. Cutting the fabric strips into rectangles as well as squares reinforces the asymmetrical look of these quilts.

To prevent the necessity of partial seams during construction, the Block Set Guides for the 2" grid (pages 55–58) are split into columns. See FANGS 2 U (page 28) and SUGAR & SPICE (page18) for details.

How many fabrics to use? A good question! I have used as few as six and as many as 25. Using 10–12 fabrics will give a good mix without too many repeats.

## Fabric Requirements

|  | Baby | Throw | Twin | Queen |
|---|---|---|---|---|
| T-shirts* | 15–19 | 10-15 | 15–19 | 20-25 |
| Iron-on interfacing | 3 yards | 8 yards | 10 yards | 13 yards |
| Various fabrics for squares |  | 1⅔ yards | 2¼ yards | 3⅓ yards |
| Inner border | ⅓ yard | ½ yard | ½ yard | ⅔ yard |
| Outer border and binding | 1¼ yards | 2⅓ yards | 2⅔ yards | 3 yards |

*If you are using images from both the front and back, you'll need fewer T-shirts.

## Construction

Stabilize your T-shirts as instructed in Cutting and Stabilizing T-Shirts (page 7).

Trim the T's to block dimensions appropriate for your chosen grid size. If a motif lends itself to a circular or oval shape, refer to Incorporating Curves into T-Shirt Quilts (page 10).

Note the size of each T-shirt block in the appropriate Cut Block Chart (pages 50–53). Calculate and cut the number of fabric squares needed.

If you have Electric Quilt 7 software, construct a grid to plan your layout.

If you do not have design software, use one of the Block Set Guides (pages 55–61) in the Easy Planning Guides chapter to plan your layout.

# Grid Method Quilts

Audition the placement of the T-shirt blocks in your design layout. At this point in the design process I do not worry about which T-shirt goes where but rather where specific sizes of T-shirts are placed. Remember, this is an asymmetrical design. The T-shirt blocks should look like they were placed randomly.

In this example, the white squares represent fabric Charm Squares while the various T-shirt block sizes are differentiated by color.

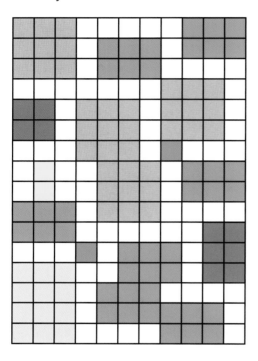

In an optimum placement, the area occupied by T-shirts as compared to fabric squares is about 55–62 percent. Use data from the Cut Block Chart if you want to figure the percentage in your own layout (page 52). If math is not your thing, having 3–7 T-shirt sides touching another T-shirt provides a good visual balance for quilts up to twin size; 12 touches for queen size when using a 6" grid. In CHARMED JOURNEY for example on page 24, T-shirt sides touch other T-shirts 5 times. The Block Set Guide is just that—a guide. There is no hard and fast rule for the exact size of any quilt. Vary the block set to optimize the fabric-to-T-shirts ratio.

Lay out your T-shirt blocks and fabric squares on a design wall, following your Block Set Guide. This is the time for auditioning which T-shirt is placed where in the design. Try to mix the light and dark values when determining the placement of T-shirt blocks. You want your eye to travel around the quilt, not have it drawn to a specific area.

Once you have finalized your arrangement, sew fabric squares and T-shirt blocks together into sections, pressing seams away from the T-shirts. Press fabric-to-fabric seams in the direction that will create nestled seams when subsections are sewn to a T-shirt. Sew sections together to complete the top.

Measure through the center of the quilt in both directions to determine the length needed for the borders.

Cut 2" wide strips for the inner border and 6½" wide strips for the outer border. Attach the borders to the quilt top.

Quilt as desired.

University of Texas M. D. Anderson Cancer Center
©2011, Texas A&M University
Jenalia Moreno www.stitchedfilm.com
Katy Independent School District, Katy, Texas

# Scavenger Hunt

65" x 86", made by the author, quilted by Quilt 'N Sew Studio, Katy, Texas

Another example of a quilt constructed with the Grid Method.

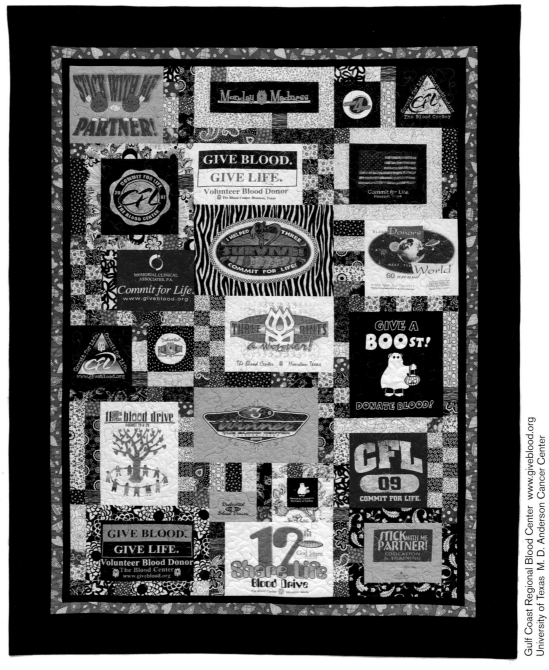

# Fangs 2 U

66" x 86", made by the author

This 2" Grid Method quilt is Jelly Roll friendly. A column construction method is used on this smaller grid to prevent the occurrence of partial seams. This is another great design method for incorporating T-shirt blocks of differing dimensions into a quilt.

## Fabric Requirements

|  | Twin | Full/Queen |
|---|---|---|
| *T-shirts | 15–19 | 20–25 |
| Iron-on interfacing ½ yard per shirt | 10 yards | 13 yards |
| Precut 2½" black-and-white WOF strips | 21 | 32 |
| 2½" red squares from various fabrics | 34 | 45 |
| Inner border | ⅓ yard | ½ yard |
| Middle border | ½ yard | ⅔ yard |
| Outer border and binding | 2⅔ yards | 3 yards |

*If you are using images from both the front and back, you'll need fewer T-shirts.

## Quilt Construction

For the checkerboard squares, make 2 strip-sets with a predominately black and predominately white precut 2½" WOF strip each. Press toward the darker strip. Cut into 2½" segments.

Cut 12 (twin) or 17 (full/queen) WOF strips into the number and sizes of segments indicated, cutting with the largest segments first. Reserve the remaining WOF strips for later.

| Segment Length | Segments for Twin | Segments for Full/Queen |
|---|---|---|
| 12½" | 3 | 5 |
| 10½" | 3 | 5 |
| 8½" | 5 | 7 |
| 6½" | 25 | 35 |
| 4½" | 27 | 36 |
| 2½" | 30 | 40 |

Stabilize the T-shirts as instructed in Cutting and Stabilizing T-Shirts (see page 7). Trim the T-shirts to dimensions divisible by 2 plus ½" (2½", 4½", 6½", 8½", etc.), whichever dimensions are appropriate for each shirt.

Note the size of each T-shirt block in the 2" Cut Block Chart (page 50).

Divide the T-shirt blocks into 3 groups. Plan to place wider T-shirt blocks in the center column.

If you have Electric Quilt 7 software, construct a three-column grid to plan your layout. (To change EQ7's default setting of 24 blocks, click on the Quilt tab, then Quilt Worktable Options/Layout Options/All Styles to increase the maximum number of blocks.)

If you do not have design software, use a 2" Grid Block Set Guide (pages 55–58) to plan your layout. Audition placement of the T-shirt blocks in the design. Remember this is a guide; adjust the block set as appropriate for your T-shirt collection.

Here is the Block Set Guide I used for Fangs 2 U.

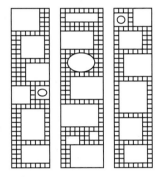

Following your Block Set Guide, place the T-shirt blocks on a design surface and audition placement of the cut fabric segments. To camouflage the column construction, position checkerboard segments on either side of the column breaks, being careful to continue the light/dark pattern. Intersperse the black-and-white segments with red fabric squares. Cut reserve strips as desired to complete a pleasing layout.

Sew fabrics and T-shirt blocks together to create each column. Press the seam allowance away from the T-shirts when joining fabrics to T-shirts. Press fabric-to-fabric seams in the direction that will create nestled seams when subsections are sewn together.

Sew the columns together.

Measure through the center of quilt in both directions to determine the length for the borders. Cut 1½" wide strips for the first border. Cut 2" wide strips for the second border. Cut 5½" wide strips for the third border. Add the borders to complete the quilt top.

Quilt as desired.

# Split Formation

67" x 88", made by the author

This Cinderella quilt appears much more complicated than its humble Nine-Patch block beginnings. A very big bang for the buck! All the T-shirt blocks need to be the same size.

You need 3 Nine-Patch blocks for a twin size top (67" x 85") and 4 for a queen (89" x 89").

## Fabric Requirements

|  | Twin | Queen |
|---|---|---|
| T-shirts* | 12 | 16 |
| Iron-on interfacing | 6 yards | 8 yards |
| 12½" squares of various black-and-white fabrics | 12 | 16 |
| Nine-Patch Centers (blue) | ½ yard | ⅞ yard |
| Inner border | ⅝ yard | ⅞ yard |
| Outer border and binding | 2½ yards | 2½ yards |

*If you are using images from both the front and back, you'll need fewer T-shirts.

## Quilt Construction

Stabilize the T-shirts as instructed in Cutting and Stabilizing T-Shirts (see page 7) and trim each to measure 12½" x 12½".

Cut 3 (twin) or 4 (queen) 12½" x 12½" squares from blue fabric for Nine-Patch centers.

Audition placement of 4 T-shirts, 4 black-and-white squares, and one blue square for each Nine-Patch block. Don't overly obsess when determining placement; the look of their placement will be altered when the blocks are sliced and rearranged.

For the twin, make 2 Nine-Patch blocks with the T-shirt images all right-side up (figure 1) and one Nine-Patch block with the bottom two T-shirt images upside-down (figure 2).

For the queen-size quilt, make 4 Nine-Patch blocks with the images all right-side up (figure 1).

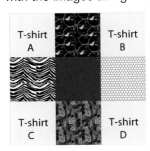

**Figure 1**          **Figure 2**

Before cutting the Nine-Patch blocks into sub-blocks, label each block as shown (figure 3).

Cut the Nine-Patch blocks into 4 sub-blocks (figure 4).

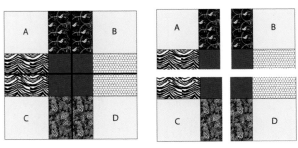

**Figure 3**          **Figure 4**

Use 2 rulers to find the center of the block, remove one ruler, and slice the block in half vertically. Repeat on the horizontal.

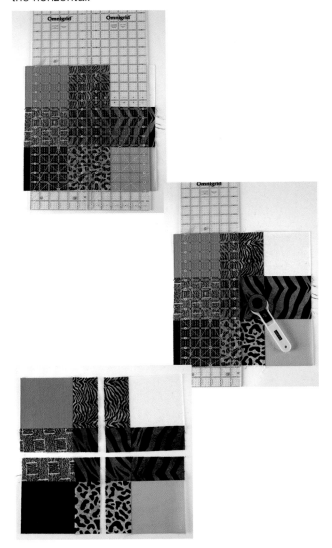

# Split Formation

Arrange the blocks as shown.

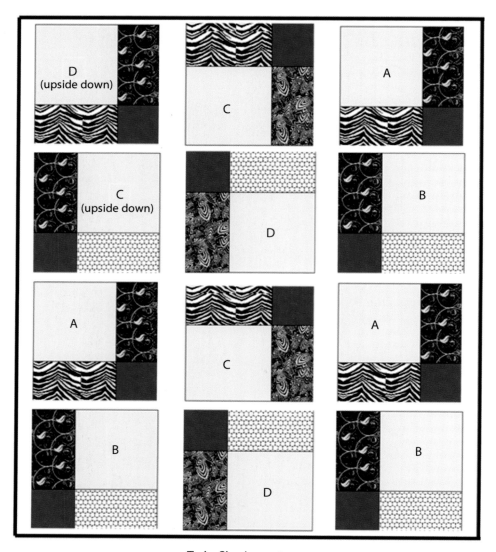

Twin-Size Layout

Sew the blocks into rows, pressing the seams in opposite directions in alternate rows.

Sew the rows together, pressing the seams in one direction.

Measure through the center of the quilt in both directions to determine the length needed for the borders.

Cut 2" wide strips for the inner border. Cut 6½" wide strips for the outer border. Attach the borders to complete the quilt top.

Quilt as desired.

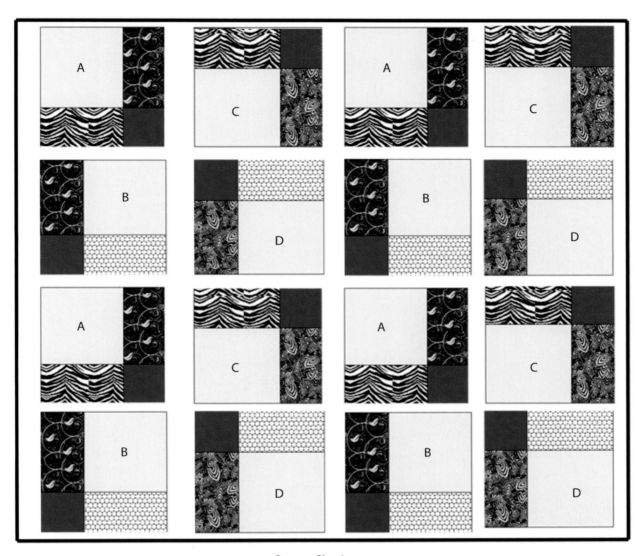

Queen-Size Layout

Katy Independent School District, Katy, Texas
First United Methodist Church in Katy, Texas
Gulf Coast Regional Blood Center www.giveblood.org
Zeta Tau Alpha www.zetataualpha.org
Holy Covenant United Methodist Church in Carrollton, Texas

# Safari Sashed

60" x 73", made by the author, quilted by Quilt 'N Sew Studio, Katy, Texas

This traditional T-shirt quilt construction method requires all T-shirt blocks to be the same size. See Design Opportunities (page 14) for methods of incorporating odd sized T-shirts. To make a Cinderella quilt using this method, the design needs to include borders with fabric that makes a strong statement.

## Fabric Requirements

| Size | T-Shirts* | Sashing Segments | Sashing Yardage | WOF Strips | Cornerstone Yardage | # Cornerstone WOF Strips | Cornerstones | Inner Border | Outer Border & Binding |
|---|---|---|---|---|---|---|---|---|---|
| Throw | 12 | 31 | 1¼ yards | 11 | ½ yard | 2 | 20 | ½ yard | 2⅓ yards |
| Dorm Twin | 24 | 58 | 2 yards | 20 | ½ yard | 3 | 35 | | |
| Dorm w/ Border | 15 | 38 | 1¼ yards | 13 | ½ yard | 2 | 24 | ½ yard | 2⅔ yards |
| Queen | 36 | 82 | 2½ yards | 28 | ½ yard | 4 | 49 | | |
| Queen w/ Border | 25 | 60 | 2 yards | 20 | ½ yard | 3 | 36 | ⅔ yard | 3 yards |

*If you are using images from both the front and back, you'll need fewer T-shirts.

## Quilt Construction

Cut sashing segments 3" x 12½" from the WOF strips.

Cut cornerstones 3" x 3".

Stabilize the T-shirts as instructed in Cutting and Stabilizing T-Shirts (page 7).

Using a 12½" square ruler, trim the T-shirts into blocks measuring 12½" x 12½".

Lay out the T-shirt blocks, sashing segments, and cornerstones on a design surface and audition the placement of the T-shirt blocks. Try to mix the light and dark values. You want your eye to travel around the quilt, not have it drawn to a specific area.

Using a ¼" seam allowance, sew the sashings, cornerstones, and blocks into vertical columns. Press the seams toward the sashing.

Sew the columns together.

Measure through the center of the quilt in both directions to determine the length for the borders.

Cut the inner borders 2" wide.

For the throw quilt, cut the outer borders 5½" wide. For the bed-size quilts, cut the outer borders 6½" wide.

Add the borders to complete the quilt top.

Quilt as desired.

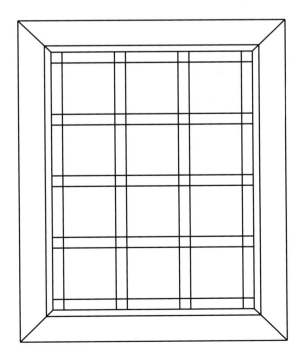

Amy Bradley Designs  www.amybradleydesigns.com
Benartex  www.benartex.com
Greater Houston Area Shop Hop
Block Party Studios  www.blockpartystudios.com
Quilter's Guild of Dallas

# Twistin' Fun

63" x 79", made by the author, quilted by Quilt 'N Sew Studio, Katy, Texas

This is a great method to use when your T-shirts vary slightly in size.

## Fabric Requirements

12 T-shirts*

6 yards iron-on interfacing, ½ yard per shirt

12 – $^1/_3$ yard cuts assorted prints (4 yards total)

½ yard for the inner border

2$^1/_3$ yards for the outer border & binding

*If you are using images from both the front and back, you'll need fewer T-shirts.

Special tools for this project: 16½" square ruler

## Quilt Construction

Stabilize the T-shirts as instructed in Cutting and Stabilizing T-Shirts (page 7).

Center each image under a 12½" square ruler and trim the shirts to measure 12½" x 12½".

**Note: Sizes can vary slightly. The largest shirts in this quilt were cut 13¼".**

Pair each T-shirt with a print fabric. Cut 2–4½" wide WOF strips from each print fabric. Subcut a 12½" segment and a 20½" segment from each strip (4 segments total). Adjust the cut segment lengths for any T-shirt larger than 12½" x 12½".

Sew print strips to the sides of each T-shirt block as shown.

Press seams away from the T-shirt.

Position a 16½" square ruler on a block, twisting it to the **left**. Trim around all 4 sides. Repeat with 5 more blocks.

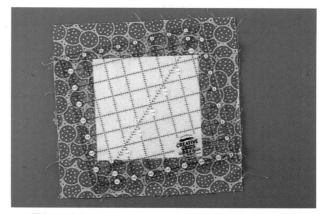

*Trim 6 blocks with the ruler twisted to the left.*

Trim the remaining blocks with the ruler twisted to the **right**.

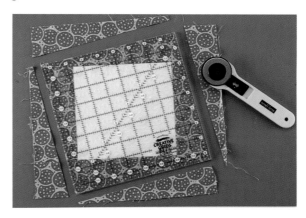

*Trim 6 blocks with the ruler twisted to the right.*

Arrange the blocks in 4 rows of 3 blocks each, alternating the angle of the T-shirt image.

Sew the blocks into rows. Press the seams in opposite directions on alternate rows.

Join the rows together, pressing the seams in the same direction.

Cut 2" wide strips for the inner border. Cut 6½" strips from the outer border. Attach the borders to complete the quilt top.

Quilt as desired.

# T-Shirt Memory Pillow

20" x 26", made by the author

Use this classic Courthouse Steps block with a 6" x 12" (finished) T-shirt block to make a standard bed pillow sham (20" x 26") or use a 12" square (finished) block to make a 24" square dorm-size pillow.

Because the Courthouse Steps block is in the Log Cabin block family, the rectangular fabric shapes are commonly referred to as "logs."

## Fabric Requirements

| Logs (for either size) | 3 – ¼ yard cuts of coordinating fabrics OR 12 WOF strips up to 4" wide |
|---|---|
| Backing for standard sham | ½ yard. Cut into 2 – 16" x 20½" rectangles. |
| Backing for dorm pillow | ¾ yard. Cut into 2 – 15" x 24½" rectangles. |
| Iron-on interfacing | ½ yard |

Additional supplies: 24" x 24" pillow form if you're making the dorm pillow

## Pillow Construction

Cut logs for your pillow as indicated in the chart below:

| Step | 20" x 26" Pillow Sham | 24" Dorm Pillow |
|---|---|---|
| 1a | 2 – 2" x 12½" | 2 – 1½" x 12½" |
| b | 2 – 2" x 9½" | 2 – 1½" x 14½" |
| 2a | 2 – 3" x 15½" | 2 – 2¼" x 14½" |
| b | 2 – 3" x 14½" | 2 – 2¼" x 18" |
| 3a | 4 – 3½" x 20½" | 2 – 3¾" x 18" |
| b | | 2 – 3¾" x 24½" |

Stabilize your T-shirt as instructed in Cutting and Stabilizing T-Shirts (page 7). Trim the T-shirt image to measure 6½" x 12½" (sham) or 12½" x 12½" (dorm pillow).

Topstitch the stabilized T-shirt block as shown in Finishing Touches (page 15).

Sew the logs to the T-shirt block using a ¼" seam allowance.

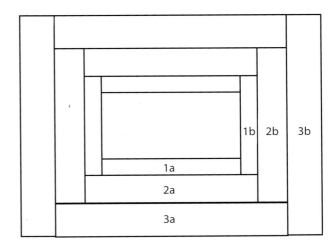

For the back of the pillow, press under one long edge of both rectangles ½". Fold again and press, creating a hem. Topstitch in place.

With right sides together, pin the pillow backs to the pillow top, overlapping the hemmed edges (by about 3"). Sew around all 4 sides with a ½" seam allowance.

If you'd like rounded corners, use a plastic cup or glass and marking tool to draw curves at the corners. Sew on the marked lines. Trim the seams and clip the seam allowance close to the seam lines.

Turn the pillow cover right side out, and insert the pillow.

# Gallery

Plano Youth Soccer, Plano, Texas
North Texas Soccer
Quickfoot Tournament Series www.quickfoot.com

© 2011, Texas A&M University
Plano Independent School District, Plano, Texas

## ISN'T THAT DARLING!

87" x 94", made by the author, quilted by Quilt 'N Sew Studio, Katy, Texas

**HOTTEST BRAND RUNNING**

80" x 90", made by Debra North, Katy, Texas,
quilted by Pam Klein, Katy, Texas

ConocoPhillips www.conocophillips.com

### FROGS AND SNAILS AND PUPPY-DOGS' TAILS

35" x 42", made by the author

## JUSTIN'S T-SHIRT QUILT

60" x 90", made by the author.

From the collection of Justin Bauman, Fulshear, Texas.

**SERENDIPITY**

65" x 86", made by the author

Amy Bradley Designs www.
amybradleydesigns.com
Dinosaur Land in Vernal, Utah

Colgate-Palmolive Company
©2011, Texas A&M University
Katy Independent School District, Katy, Texas

Missoula Children's Theatre in Missoula, Montana www.mctinc.org
Airbrushing by student Aaron Goodman

Community Christian Academy in Paducah, Kentucky
Paducah Public Schools in Paducah, Kentucky
Upward Basketball www.upward.org

## LEIGH'S QUILT

58" x 91", made by Lynn Loyd, Cheryl Perilloux, and Jane Walker,
Paducah, Kentucky

Community Christian Academy in Paducah, Kentucky
McCracken County Public Schools in Paducah, Kentucky
US Space & Rocket Center www.spacecamp.com

Christian County Public Schools Schools in Hopkinsville, Kentucky
Union University in Jackson, Tennessee
Atomic Airbrush www.atomicairbrush.com

## RYAN'S QUILT

48" x 71", made by Cheryl Perilloux, Yvonne Robinson, and Jane Walker,
Paducah, Kentucky

## QUILT CITY

65" x 86", made by Linda Baxter Lasco, Paducah, Kentucky

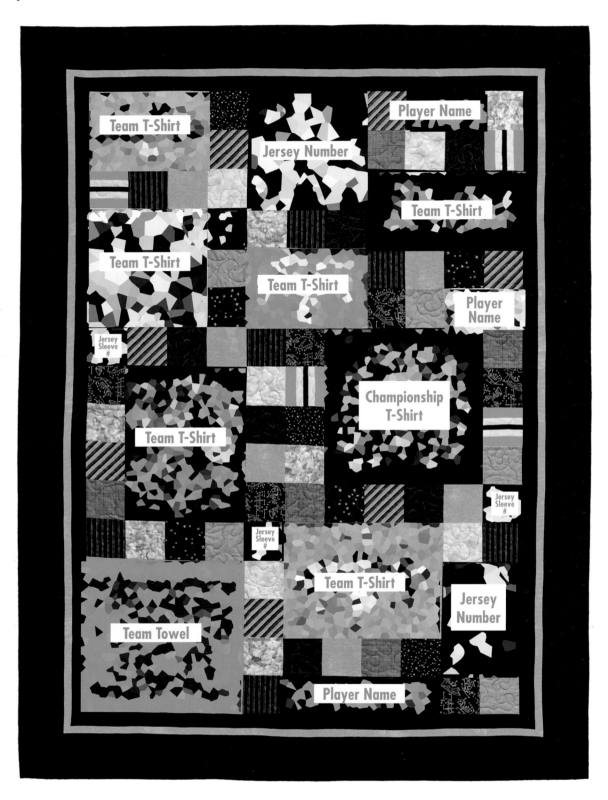

## SPORTS TEAM QUILT

57" x 77", made by the author

# Easy Planning Guides
## Comparing the Quilt Designs

What kind of project are you making? Do you have a variety of T-shirt image sizes? Do you have loads of T-shirts or not so many? Are you using precut fabrics? Use this summary of the quilts presented to select which project design best fits your T-shirt collection.

**Comparative Quilt Design Chart**

|  | JUNIOR TWIST | Baby 2" Grid SUGAR & SPICE | Baby Split 9-Patch LOGAN'S SHIRTS OF FIRSTS | TWISTIN' FUN | 2" Grid FANGS 2 U | Split Nine-Patch SPLIT FORMATION | Standard Sashing SAFARI SASHED | 4" or 6" Grid multiple examples | Charm Square (5" cut) Grid CHARMED JOURNEY |
|---|---|---|---|---|---|---|---|---|---|
| Same size T-shirt blocks |  |  | X |  |  | X | X |  |  |
| T-shirt blocks can vary slightly | X |  |  | X |  |  |  |  |  |
| Multiple T-shirt block sizes |  | X |  |  | X |  |  | X | X |
| Precut fabric friendly | X | X | X |  | X |  |  |  | X |
| Many T-shirts needed |  |  |  |  |  |  | X |  |  |
| Fewer T-shirts needed |  |  |  |  |  | X |  |  |  |

# Cut Block Charts

Select the chart in the grid size of your quilt. Note the number of T-shirts you have in each block size in column D. From that you can figure how many grid squares the T-shirts will occupy in your quilt. Then you can tell how many grid squares of fabric pieces you'll need to complete your top.

## 2" Grid Cut Block Chart

| A | B | C | D | E |
|---|---|---|---|---|
| Cut Block Dimensions (in inches) | Block Set within Grid | # Grid Squares per Block | # T-Shirts | Total Grid Squares per Block Size (C x D = E) |
| 14½ x 14½ | 7 x 7 | 49 | | |
| 14½ x 12½ | 7 x 6 | 42 | | |
| 12½ x 14½ | 6 x 7 | 42 | | |
| 12½ x 12½ | 6 x 6 | 36 | | |
| 12½ x 10½ | 6 x 5 | 30 | | |
| 10½ x 12½ | 5 x 6 | 30 | | |
| 10½ x 10½ | 5 x 5 | 25 | | |
| 10½ x 8½ | 5 x 4 | 20 | | |
| 8½ x 10½ | 4 x 5 | 20 | | |
| 8½ x 8½ | 4 x 4 | 16 | | |
| 8½ x 6½ | 4 x 3 | 12 | | |
| 6½ x 8½ | 3 x 4 | 12 | | |
| 6½ x 6½ | 3 x 3 | 9 | | |
| 6½ x 4½ | 3 x 2 | 6 | | |
| 4½ x 6½ | 2 x 3 | 6 | | |

Note the number of T-shirts you have in each block size in column D. From that you can figure how many grid squares the T-shirts will occupy in your quilt. Then you can tell how many grid squares of fabric pieces you'll need to complete your top.

## 4" Grid Cut Block Chart

| A | B | C | D | E |
|---|---|---|---|---|
| Cut Block Dimensions (in inches) | Block Set within Grid | # Grid Squares per Block | # T-Shirts | Total Grid Squares per Block Size (C x D = E) |
| 16½ x 16½ | 4 x 4 | 16 | | |
| 16½ x 12½ | 4 x 3 | 12 | | |
| 12½ x 16½ | 3 x 4 | 12 | | |
| 16½ x 8½ | 4 x 2 | 8 | | |
| 8½ x 16½ | 2 x 4 | 8 | | |
| 16½ x 4½ | 4 x 1 | 4 | | |
| 4½ x 16½ | 1 x 4 | 4 | | |
| 12½ x 12½ | 3 x 3 | 9 | | |
| 12½ x 8½ | 3 x 2 | 6 | | |
| 8½ x 12½ | 2 x 3 | 6 | | |
| 12½ x 4½ | 3 x 1 | 3 | | |
| 4½ x 12½ | 1 x 3 | 3 | | |
| 8½ x 8½ | 2 x 2 | 4 | | |
| 8½ x 4½ | 2 x 1 | 2 | | |
| 4½ x 48½ | 1 x 2 | 2 | | |
| 4½ x 4½ | 1 x 1 | 1 | | |

# Cut Block Charts

Note the number of T-shirts you have in each block size in column D. From that you can figure how many grid squares the T-shirts will occupy in your quilt. Then you can tell how many grid squares of fabric pieces you'll need to complete your top.

## 5" Grid (Charm Square) Cut Block Chart

| A | B | C | D | E |
|---|---|---|---|---|
| Cut Block Dimensions (in inches) | Block Set within Grid | # Grid Squares per Block | # T-Shirts | Total Grid Squares per Block Size (C x D = E) |
| 18½ x 14 | 4 x 3 | 12 | | |
| 14 x 18½ | 3 x 4 | 12 | | |
| 18½ x 9½ | 4 x 2 | 8 | | |
| 9½ x 18½ | 2 x 4 | 8 | | |
| 18½ x 5 | 4 x 1 | 4 | | |
| 5 x 18½ | 1 x 4 | 4 | | |
| 14 x14 | 3 x 3 | 9 | | |
| 14 x 9½ | 3 x 2 | 6 | | |
| 9½ x 14 | 2 x 3 | 6 | | |
| 14 x 5 | 3 x 1 | 3 | | |
| 5 x 14 | 1 x 3 | 3 | | |
| 9½ x 9½ | 2 x 2 | 4 | | |
| 9½ x 5 | 2 x 1 | 2 | | |
| 5 x 9½ | 1 x 2 | 2 | | |
| 5 x 5 | 1 x 1 | 1 | | |

Note the number of T-shirts you have in each block size in column D. From that you can figure how many grid squares the T-shirts will occupy in your quilt. Then you can tell how many grid squares of fabric pieces you'll need to complete your top.

## 6" Grid Cut Block Chart

| A | B | C | D | E |
|---|---|---|---|---|
| Cut Block Dimensions (in inches) | Block Set within Grid | # Grid Squares per Block | # T-Shirts | Total Grid Squares per Block Size (C x D = E) |
| 18½ x 18½ | 3 x 3 | 9 | | |
| 18½ x 12½ | 3 x 2 | 6 | | |
| 12½ x 18½ | 2 x 3 | 6 | | |
| 18½ x 6½ | 3 x 1 | 3 | | |
| 6½ x 18½ | 1 x 3 | 3 | | |
| 12½ x 6½ | 2 x 1 | 2 | | |
| 6½ x 12½ | 1 x 2 | 2 | | |
| 6½ x 6½ | 1 x 1 | 1 | | |

## Let's Do the Numbers

In an optimum arrangement, the T-shirt area should be about 55–62% of the entire layout.

If math is not your thing, having 3–7 T-shirt sides touching another T-shirt is a good indicator of a nice visual balance for quilts up to twin size. For a 6" grid queen-size quilt, about 12 touches provide a good balance.

However, if you would like to figure your percentage, this is how.

First, you need the total number of grid squares in your quilt top (not including borders).

Use the number of squares in the width and length given in the Block Set Guides (pages 55–61) for the grid size you've selected. Multiply the number of squares in the length by the number of squares in the width to get the total number of grid squares.

(squares in length) x (squares in width) = Total # squares in quilt (S)

_____ x _____ = (S)_____

Next, find how much of your layout area is accounted for by the T-shirt blocks. Multiply the number of grid squares each size fills (column C) by the number of T-shirt blocks you have in that size (column D).

Add all the column D results for the total number of grid squares represented by your T-shirt blocks.

(C)_____ x (D)_____ = (E total)_____

Subtract the E total from the overall quilt size (S) for the number of grid squares in your overall design to be filled with fabric.

(total # squares in quilt) - (total squares filled by T-shirt blocks) = # fabric squares (F)

(S)_____ - (E total)_____ = (F)_____

To determine the percentage of T-shirt blocks in your quilt, divide the total number of squares filled by T-shirts (E) by the total number of squares in the quilt (S), then multiply by 100 for the percentage.

(Total squares T-shirt blocks occupy) ÷ (total # squares in quilt) x 100 = % area T-shirts occupy

(E total)_____ ÷ (S)_____ x 100 = _____%

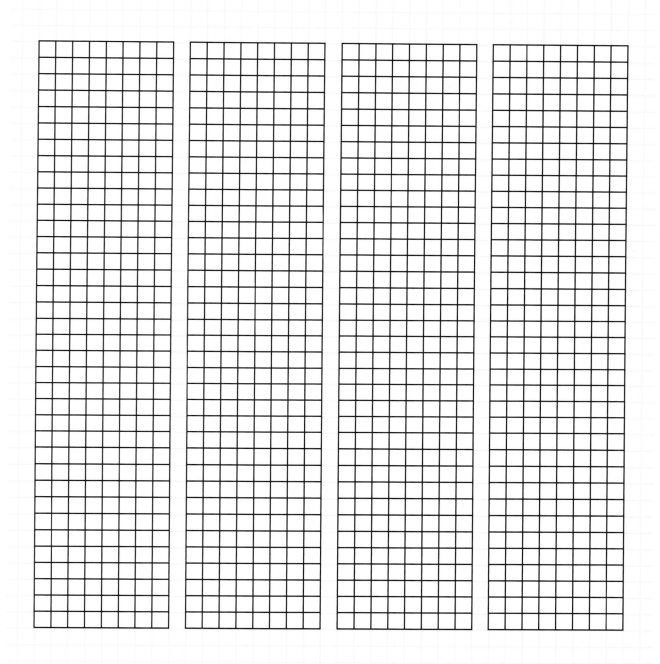

2" Grid Block Set Guide
Full Size

Columns are 16" finished.
Dimensions assume finished border sizes of 1½" and 6".

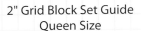

2" Grid Block Set Guide
Queen Size

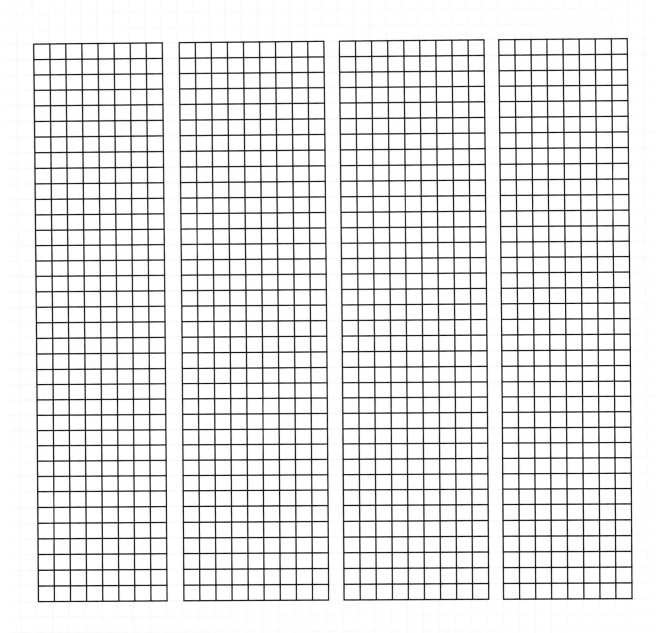

Center columns are 18" finished; outside columns are 16" finished.
Dimensions assume finished border sizes of 1½" and 6".

2" Grid Block Set Guide
Twin Size

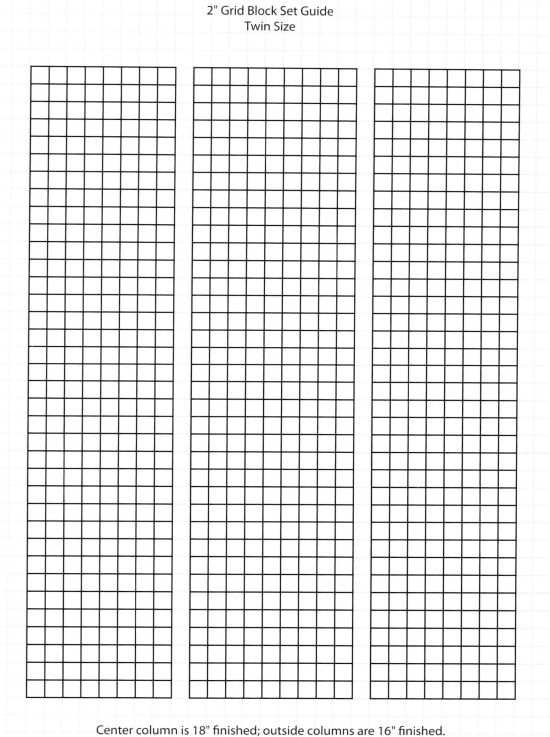

Center column is 18" finished; outside columns are 16" finished.
Dimensions assume finished border sizes of 1½" and 6".

# Block Set Guides

Baby 2" Grid Block Set Guide

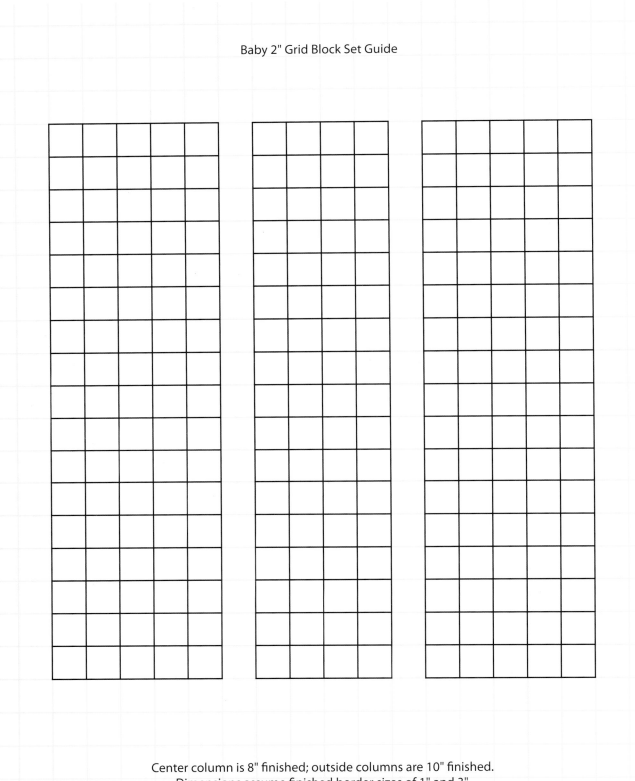

Center column is 8" finished; outside columns are 10" finished.
Dimensions assume finished border sizes of 1" and 3".

4" Grid Block Set Guide

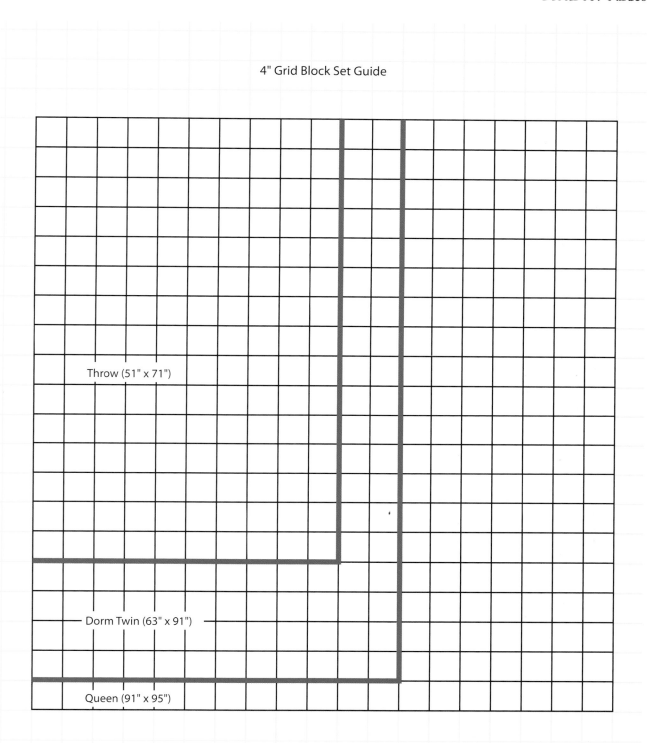

Throw (51" x 71")

Dorm Twin (63" x 91")

Queen (91" x 95")

Dimensions assume finished borders as follows:
• Throw size: 1½" and 4" borders
• Bed sizes: 1½" and 6" borders

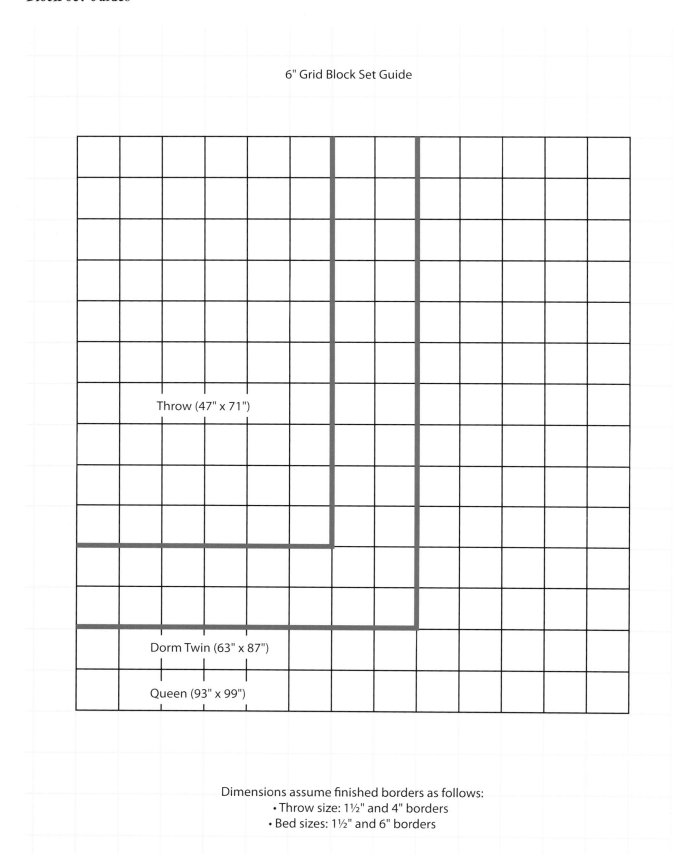

6" Grid Block Set Guide

Throw (47" x 71")

Dorm Twin (63" x 87")

Queen (93" x 99")

Dimensions assume finished borders as follows:
• Throw size: 1½" and 4" borders
• Bed sizes: 1½" and 6" borders

Charm Square 5" Grid Block Set Guide

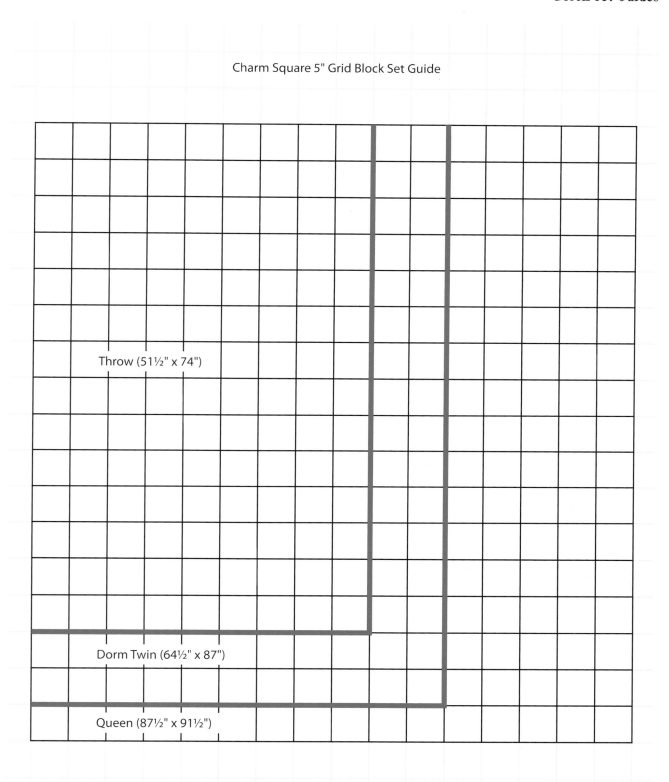

Throw (51½" x 74")

Dorm Twin (64½" x 87")

Queen (87½" x 91½")

Dimensions assume finished borders as follow:
• Throw size: 1½" and 4" borders
• Bed sizes: 1½" and 6" borders

# Resources

## Books

Hill, Wendy. *Easy Bias-Covered Curves: Create Quilts with WOW Appeal (Fast, Fun & Easy)*. Lafayette, California: C&T Publishing, 2006.

Hughes, Rose. *Dream Landscapes: Artful Quilts with Fast-Piece Appliqué*. Bothell, Washington: That Patchwork Place, 2008.

Masopust, Katie Pasquini. *Design Explorations for the Creative Quilter: Easy-to-Follow Lessons for Dynamic Art Quilts*. Lafayette, California: C&T Publishing, 2008.

Schamber, Sharon. *Piec-liqué: Curves the New Way*. Paducah, Kentucky: AQS Publishing, 2005.

## Tools, Fabrics, Notions, and Such

Aurifil™ thread, 50 weight (orange spool)
Red Rock Threads
www.redrockthreads.com

Bear Thread Designs: The Appliqué Pressing Sheet 13" x 17"
http://www.bearthreaddesigns.com

Bo-Nash Ironslide Iron Shoe
www.bonash.com

Clover® Bias Tape Maker—½" #12, (yellow—either style)
www.clover-usa.com

911FF Pellon® Fusible Featherweight
www.pellonideas.com

Warm & Natural® Needled Cotton Batting
www.warmcompany.com

# About the Author

Photo by Angela Rodgers

Martha DeLeonardis is an internationally known, award-winning quilt artist who grew up in Cincinnati, Ohio. She graduated from Ohio University in 1981 with a BS in chemical engineering. Martha worked in industry for six years before retiring to stay at home with her two sons.

Martha has been sewing since she can remember. In the second grade, she was making her own clothes under her mother's tutelage, an expert seamstress herself. Martha started quilting in 1995 when her children were young and her family lived in a small town in Ohio. She became seriously involved in this art form after moving to Katy, Texas, in 2000. She has been greatly influenced by the quilting community in the greater Houston area.

Martha has had numerous quilts juried into national and international competitions, winning a blue ribbon in 2008 at the Houston International Quilt Festival. She was also a finalist in The National Quilt Museum's Sunflower: New Quilts from Old Favorite contest in 2010 and is featured in the companion book by the same name.

Visit Martha's website at www.marthadzines.com

# More AQS Books

This is only a small selection of the books available from the AQS books are known worldwide for timely topics, clear writing, beautiful color photos and patterns. The following books are available from your local bookseller, quilt shop, or public library.

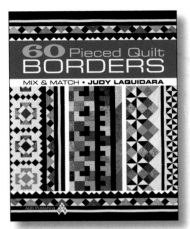

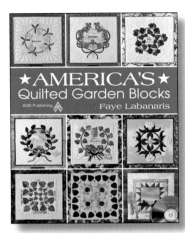

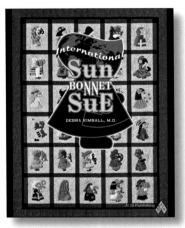

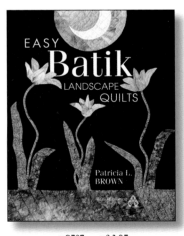